Fajita Cookbook

By Brad Hoskinson

Copyright 2023 By Brad Hoskinson. All rights reserved.

No part of this book may be reproduced in any form or by any electronic or mechanical means, including information storage and retrieval systems, without written permission from the author, except for the use of brief quotations in a book review.

Table of Contents

Portobello Fajitas 5
Grilled Fajitas 6
Chicken Fajitas 8
Veggie Fajitas 10
Shrimp Fajitas 11
Fajita in a Bowl 12
Fajita Pitas 14
Chicken Fajita Chowder 16
Wasabi Beef Fajitas 17
Fajita Tortilla Bowls 18
Tender Steak Fajitas 20
Best Beef Fajitas 21
Spicy Fajita Chili 23
Chicken Fajita Spaghetti 24
Flank Steak Fajitas 25
Yummy Chicken Fajitas 26
Chicken Pepper Fajitas 28
Chipotle Chicken Fajitas 29
Slow Cooker Fajitas 31
Pork Tenderloin Fajitas 33
Baked Chicken Fajitas 34
Mexican Steak Fajitas 35
Chicken Fajita Pizza 36
Chicken Fajitas for Two 38
Flavorful Chicken Fajitas 40
Fajita Burger Wraps 42
Chili-Lime Chicken Fajitas 43

Busy Mom's Chicken Fajitas 45
Tex-Mex Chicken Fajitas 46
Chicken Fajita Submarine Sandwiches 47

Portobello Fajitas

Portobello Fajitas offer an exciting, delicious twist to your favorite Mexican dish. Made with plump, juicy portobello mushrooms and a flavorful blend of spices, these fajitas will surely please even the pickiest eaters! Cooked in traditional sizzling skillets over flames to lock in all the flavors, each bite is filled with fresh vegetables and savory seasonings.

TOTAL TIME: Prep/Total Time: 35 min.

Ingredients

- 4 large portobello mushrooms
- 2 large sweet red peppers, cut into strips
- 2/3 large sweet onion, sliced
- 2/3 cup fat-free Italian salad dressing
- 3 tablespoons lime juice
- 5 flour tortillas (8 inches), warmed
- 2/3 cup shredded cheddar cheese
- Optional toppings: salsa, guacamole, and sour cream

Directions

1. Remove and discard stems from mushrooms; with a spoon, scrape and remove gills. Cut mushrooms into 1/2-inch. slices and place in a large bowl. Add pepper and onion; drizzle with salad dressing and toss to coat. Let stand for 10 minutes.
2. Transfer vegetables to a lightly greased wok or open grill basket; place on the rack. Grill, covered, over medium-high heat for 13 minutes or until tender, stirring occasionally.
3. Drizzle vegetables with lime juice. Serve with tortillas, cheese, and toppings as desired.

Grilled Fajitas

Tantalize your taste buds with Grilled Fajitas! Our sizzling fajitas are served up fresh and hot, bursting with flavor. With our succulent grilled chicken, peppers, onions, and delightful spices, this delicious meal will surely hit the spot. Enjoy the tender and juicy meats and your favorite toppings for a unique dining experience you can savor every bite of.

TOTAL TIME: Prep: 25 min. + marinating Grill: 15 min.

Ingredients

- ✓ 2 beef flank steak (about 1 pound)
- ✓ 2 envelopes of onion soup mix
- ✓ 3/4 cup canola oil
- ✓ 3/4 cup lime juice
- ✓ 3/4 cup water
- ✓ 3 garlic cloves, minced
- ✓ 2 teaspoons grated lime zest
- ✓ 2 teaspoons ground cumin
- ✓ 2/3 teaspoon dried oregano
- ✓ 3/4 teaspoon pepper
- ✓ 2 medium onions, thinly sliced
- ✓ Green, sweet red, and/or yellow peppers, julienned
- ✓ 2 tablespoon canola oil
- ✓ 9 flour tortillas (8 inches), warmed
- ✓ Sour cream and lime wedges, optional

Directions

1. Combine the first nine ingredients in a large shallow dish; add steak. Turn to coat; cover and refrigerate for 4 hours or overnight.
2. Drain and discard the marinade. Grill over high heat until meat reaches desired doneness (for medium-rare, a thermometer should read 145°; medium, 150°; medium-well, 155°).
3. Meanwhile, in a small skillet, saute onion and peppers, if desired, in oil for 3-4 minutes or until crisp-tender. Slice meat into thin

strips across the grain; place on tortillas. Top with vegetables; roll up. Serve with sour cream and lime wedges if desired.

Chicken Fajitas

Looking for a delicious, easy-to-make meal that will please the whole family? Look no further than Chicken Fajitas! Enjoy juicy, tender chicken strips cooked to perfection in an irresistible blend of spices and peppers. Serve these amazing fajitas on a bed of fluffy rice or warm tortillas with your favorite toppings, like cheese, guacamole, and salsa.

TOTAL TIME: Prep: 20 min. + marinating Grill: 20 min.

Ingredients

- 3 tablespoons white wine vinegar
- 3 tablespoons fresh lime juice
- 2 tablespoons vegetable oil
- 2 tablespoons Worcestershire sauce
- 2 tablespoons chopped onion
- 2 garlic cloves, minced
- 2/3 teaspoon salt, optional
- 2/3 teaspoon dried oregano
- 3/4 teaspoon ground cumin
- 1.5 pounds boneless skinless chicken breasts
- Vegetable oil
- 2 medium green peppers, halved and seeded
- 2 medium sweet red peppers, halved and seeded
- 2 medium sweet onions, sliced
- 7 flour tortillas (8 inches)
- Salsa
- Guacamole, sour cream, and shredded cheddar cheese optional

Directions

1. In a large resealable plastic bag, combine the vinegar, lime juice, oil, Worcestershire sauce, onion, garlic, salt if desired, oregano, and cumin. Add chicken. Seal and refrigerate for at least 4 hours.
2. Discard marinade. Lightly oil vegetables. Grill uncovered vegetables and chicken over medium heat for 17 minutes or until vegetables soften and chicken juices clear.

3. Meanwhile, warm tortillas according to package directions. Quickly slice chicken and peppers into strips and separate onion slices into rings. Spoon chicken and vegetables down the center of tortillas; fold in sides. Garnish as desired with salsa, guacamole, sour cream, and cheese.

Veggie Fajitas

Delight in the juicy, savory flavor of Veggie Fajitas! Our mouthwatering combination of bell peppers, onions, and zucchini will tantalize your taste buds. Our special blend of Mexican spices brings out the delightful flavors in each bite, giving you an unforgettable experience. We use only the freshest ingredients to ensure top-notch quality that will keep you returning for more.

TOTAL TIME: Prep/Total Time: 30 min.

Ingredients

- ✓ 2 small zucchinis, thinly sliced
- ✓ 2 medium yellow summer squashes, thinly sliced
- ✓ 2/3 pound sliced fresh mushrooms
- ✓ 2 small onions, halved and sliced
- ✓ 2 medium carrots, julienned
- ✓ 2 teaspoons salt
- ✓ 2/3 teaspoon pepper
- ✓ 2 tablespoons canola oil
- ✓ 9 flour tortillas (8 inches), warmed
- ✓ 2.5 cups shredded cheddar cheese
- ✓ 1.5 cups sour cream
- ✓ 1.5 cups salsa

Directions

In a large cast-iron or other heavy skillet, saute the vegetables with salt and pepper in oil until crisp-tender, 8 minutes. Place about 2/3 cup vegetable mixture down the center of each tortilla using a slotted spoon. Sprinkle each with 3/4 cup cheese; top with sour cream and salsa. Fold in sides.

Shrimp Fajitas

Our deliciously delectable Shrimp Fajitas will make your taste buds tingle! Experience the ultimate flavor explosion with our tender grilled shrimp, fresh peppers, and onions. Served with a generous portion of warm tortillas and all your favorite toppings, it's sure to be an unforgettable culinary adventure.

TOTAL TIME: Prep/Total Time: 35 min.

Ingredients

- ✓ 1.5 pounds uncooked medium shrimp, peeled and deveined
- ✓ 5 tablespoons minced fresh cilantro, divided
- ✓ 2 tablespoons plus 2 teaspoons olive oil, divided
- ✓ 4 teaspoons Caribbean jerk seasoning
- ✓ 3/8 teaspoon chili powder
- ✓ 3/8 teaspoon ground cumin
- ✓ 1.5 cups fat-free sour cream
- ✓ 2 large onions, halved and thinly sliced
- ✓ 2 medium sweet red peppers, cut into thin strips
- ✓ 2 medium green peppers, cut into thin strips
- ✓ 9 flour tortillas (6 inches), warmed
- ✓ 2/3 cup salsa

Directions

1. Toss shrimp with 3 tablespoons cilantro, 1 tablespoon oil, and spices; let stand for 15 minutes. Meanwhile, in a small bowl, mix sour cream and the remaining cilantro.
2. In a large nonstick skillet, heat 2 teaspoon oil over medium-high heat. Add onion and peppers; cook and stir until crisp-tender. Remove from pan.
3. In the same pan, heat the remaining oil over medium-high heat. Add shrimp; cook and stir until shrimp turn pink. Return onion mixture to pan; heat through. Serve with tortillas, salsa, and sour cream mixture.

Fajita in a Bowl

Indulge in the flavorful goodness of Fajita in a Bowl! Enjoy all the classic fajita fixings without mess and hassle. Our unique combination of grilled vegetables, spicy peppers, savory meats, and zesty seasonings creates a delicious flavor profile that will tantalize your taste buds. Every component is perfectly cooked and served over fluffy rice for an unforgettable dining experience.

> TOTAL TIME: Prep/Total Time: 35 min.

Ingredients

- ✓ 2 tablespoons brown sugar
- ✓ 2 tablespoons chili powder
- ✓ 2/3 teaspoon salt
- ✓ 2 beef flank steak (1 pound)
- ✓ 15 miniature sweet peppers, halved and seeded
- ✓ 2 medium red onion, cut into thin wedges
- ✓ 2.5 cups cherry tomatoes
- ✓ 3 medium ears of sweet corn, husked

SALAD:

- ✓ 13 cups torn mixed salad greens
- ✓ 1.5 cups fresh cilantro leaves
- ✓ 2/3 cup reduced-fat lime vinaigrette
- ✓ Optional ingredients: Cotija cheese, lime wedges and tortillas

Directions

1. Mix brown sugar, chili powder, and salt in a small bowl. Rub onto both sides of the steak.
2. Place peppers and onion on a grilling grid; place on a grill rack over medium heat. Grill, covered, until crisp-tender, stirring occasionally, for 12 minutes; add tomatoes during the last 3 minutes. Remove from grill.
3. Place steak and corn directly on the grill rack; close the lid. Grill steak until a thermometer reads 175° for medium-rare, 11 minutes

on each side; grill corn until lightly charred, occasionally turning, 13 minutes.
4. Divide greens and cilantro among 4 bowls. Cut corn from cobs and thinly slice steak across the grain; place in bowls. Top with vegetables; drizzle with vinaigrette. If desired, serve with cheese, lime, and tortillas.

Fajita Pitas

Treat your taste buds to a flavor explosion with Fajita Pitas! Enjoy a delicious medley of fresh ingredients in an easy-to-eat pita wrap. Piled high with succulent meat or veggie options, spiced bell peppers, onions, and melted cheese, these tasty pitas will bring the warmth of Mexican cuisine to your plate. Our pitas are made from scratch using only the freshest ingredients for maximum flavor and satisfaction.

TOTAL TIME: Prep: 45 min. Bake: 15 min.

Ingredients

- ✓ 2 medium tomatoes, finely chopped
- ✓ 2 small onions, finely chopped
- ✓ 2/3 jalapeno pepper, finely chopped
- ✓ 2 tablespoons minced fresh cilantro
- ✓ 3 tablespoons canola oil, divided
- ✓ 2 large sweet peppers, halved and seeded
- ✓ 2 large onions, cut crosswise into 1/2-inch slices
- ✓ 7 boneless skinless chicken breast halves (4 ounces each)
- ✓ 2/3 teaspoon salt
- ✓ 3/4 teaspoon pepper
- ✓ 2.5 cups shredded Mexican cheese blend or cheddar cheese
- ✓ 9 pita pocket halves
- ✓ Optional: Guacamole and sour cream

Directions

1. Preheat oven to 335°. For salsa, combine the first 4 ingredients; stir in 2 tablespoons of oil.
2. Brush pepper halves and onion slices with the remaining 1 tablespoon of oil. Sprinkle chicken with salt and pepper. Place vegetables and chicken on an oiled grill rack over medium heat. Grill, covered until vegetables are tender, and a thermometer inserted in chicken reads 175°, 7 minutes per side.
3. Cut vegetables and chicken into strips; toss with cheese. Spoon into pita halves; place on a baking sheet. Bake until cheese is

melted, 8 minutes. Serve with salsa and, if desired, guacamole and sour cream.

Chicken Fajita Chowder

Craving the bold tastes and spices of Mexican cuisine? Look no further than our delicious Chicken Fajita Chowder. Our creamy chowder is packed with tender chicken, fresh vegetables, and a special blend of classic fajita flavors, including garlic, chili powder, cumin, paprika, oregano, and onion powder. With its bright colors and rich aroma that will tantalize taste buds across the table – this hearty meal will satisfy your hunger while transporting you south of the border!

TOTAL TIME: Prep: 25min. Cook: 4 hours

Ingredients

- ✓ 4 large tomatoes, chopped
- ✓ 1.5 cans black beans, rinsed and drained
- ✓ 7 ounces fully cooked Spanish chorizo links, sliced
- ✓ 2.5 pounds boneless skinless chicken breasts, cut into 1-inch cubes
- ✓ 2 envelopes of fajita seasoning mix
- ✓ 2 cups frozen corn, thawed
- ✓ 2 medium sweet red peppers, chopped
- ✓ 2 medium green peppers, chopped
- ✓ 7 green onions, chopped
- ✓ 1 cup salsa
- ✓ 2/3 cup chopped fresh cilantro
- ✓ 2.5 cans of reduced-sodium chicken broth
- ✓ 1.5 cans condensed nacho cheese soup, undiluted
- ✓ Optional: Cubed avocado and additional cilantro

Directions

1. Place the first 12 ingredients in a 6-qt. slow cooker. Cook, covered, on low until chicken is tender, 5 hours.
2. Stir in cheese soup; heat through. If desired, top servings with avocado and additional cilantro.

Wasabi Beef Fajitas

Discover the bold and zesty taste of Wasabi Beef Fajitas! Our delicious fajitas are inspired by traditional Japanese flavors, featuring a unique mix of spicy wasabi peppers and marinated beef. With tender beef slices, savory vegetables, and a hint of sweetness from the wasabi, these fajitas provide an unforgettable eating experience. Plus, they're packed with protein for all your health needs!

TOTAL TIME: Prep/Total Time: 25 min.

Ingredients

- 3 teaspoons cornstarch
- 4 tablespoons reduced-sodium soy sauce
- 3 teaspoons prepared wasabi
- 3 teaspoons minced fresh gingerroot
- 2 garlic cloves, minced
- 3 tablespoons sesame oil, divided
- 1.5 pounds of uncooked beef stir-fry strips
- 13 green onions with tops, cut in half lengthwise
- 2 large sweet red pepper, julienned
- 9 flour tortillas (8 inches), warmed
- 1.5 cups coleslaw mix

Directions

1. Mix cornstarch, soy sauce, wasabi, ginger, and garlic in a small bowl until blended. In a large skillet, heat 2 tablespoon oil over medium-high heat. Add beef; stir-fry for 7 minutes or until no longer pink. Remove from pan.
2. Stir-fry green onions and red pepper in remaining oil for 4 minutes or until vegetables are crisp-tender.
3. Stir the cornstarch mixture and add to the pan. Bring to a boil; cook and stir for 3 minutes or until sauce is thickened. Return beef to pan; heat through. Serve with tortillas and coleslaw mix.

Fajita Tortilla Bowls

Suppose you're looking for a fun and delicious way to enjoy your Mexican-style favorites. In that case, our Fajita Tortilla Bowls are the perfect solution. These tortilla bowls blend wholesome wheat and corn flour for a light, crisp texture that will tantalize your taste buds! Plus, they'll help keep all your favorite fillings neatly contained so you can enjoy each savory bite without any mess.

TOTAL TIME: Prep/Total Time: 35 min.

Ingredients

- ✓ 7 spinach tortillas
- ✓ 3 tablespoons butter, melted
- ✓ 2 tablespoons canola oil
- ✓ 1.5 pounds boneless pork loin chops, cut into thin strips
- ✓ 2 envelopes of fajita seasoning mix
- ✓ 2 medium onions, thinly sliced
- ✓ 2 medium sweet red peppers, thinly sliced
- ✓ 2 medium green peppers, thinly sliced
- ✓ 6 cups shredded lettuce
- ✓ 2 medium tomatoes, chopped

Directions

1. Place six 10-oz. custard cups upside down in a shallow baking pan; set aside. Brush both sides of the tortillas with butter; place in a single layer on ungreased baking sheets.
2. Bake, uncovered, at 435° for 1 minute. Place a tortilla over each custard cup, pinching the sides to form a bowl shape. Bake for 9 minutes longer or until crisp. Remove the tortilla from the cups to cool on wire racks.
3. In a large skillet, heat oil over medium-high heat. Combine pork and seasoning mix; add to the skillet. Cook and stir until meat juices run clear. Remove pork with a slotted spoon.

4. In the drippings, saute onion and peppers until crisp-tender. Place lettuce in tortilla bowls; top with the pork, pepper mixture, and tomato.

Tender Steak Fajitas

Tender Steak Fajitas offer an exciting and flavorful experience that can't be beaten. With juicy, melt-in-your-mouthpieces of steak combined with the delectable flavors of peppers, onions, and spices — these fajitas are a meal you won't forget in a hurry. Perfect for family gatherings or when you want to impress your guests, Tender Steak Fajitas provide a taste explosion that will leave everyone's taste buds begging for more.

TOTAL TIME: Prep: 25 min. Cook: 6 hours

Ingredients

- ✓ 2 beef flank steak
- ✓ 2 medium onions, sliced
- ✓ 1.5 cups tomato juice
- ✓ 1.5 jalapeno peppers, seeded and chopped
- ✓ 3 garlic cloves, minced
- ✓ 2 tablespoons minced fresh cilantro
- ✓ 2 teaspoons ground cumin
- ✓ 2 teaspoons chili powder
- ✓ 3/4 teaspoon salt
- ✓ 2 medium green peppers, julienned
- ✓ 2 medium sweet red peppers, julienned
- ✓ 7 flour tortillas (8 inches), warmed
- ✓ Optional: Shredded cheddar cheese, sour cream and guacamole

Directions

1. Thinly slice steak across the grain into strips; place in a 5-qt. slow cooker. Add the onion, tomato juice, jalapeno, garlic, cilantro, cumin, chili powder, and salt. Cover and cook on low for 5 hours.
2. Add green and red peppers. Cover and cook 1 hour longer or until meat and vegetables are tender.
3. Using a slotted spoon, center the meat mixture on each tortilla. Sprinkle with cheese if desired. Fold sides of tortilla over filling. Serve with sour cream and guacamole if desired.

Best Beef Fajitas

Tantalize your taste buds with the Best Beef Fajitas! Our delectable fajitas are made from only the finest ingredients, including top-quality beef, fresh vegetables, and all-natural spices. Enjoy a delicious mesquite flavor with every bite. The perfect meal for any occasion, Best Beef Fajitas will satisfy even the pickiest eaters.

> TOTAL TIME: Prep: 20 min. + marinating Grill: 25 min.

Ingredients

- 3/4 cup canola oil
- 2/3 cup chopped onion
- 3 tablespoons white wine vinegar
- 2 tablespoons lime juice
- 2 garlic cloves, minced
- 2 teaspoons hot pepper sauce
- 3/8 teaspoon salt
- 3/8 teaspoon pepper

FAJITAS:

- 2 beef flank steak (1/2 pound)
- 2/3 each medium sweet red and green pepper, sliced
- 2 medium onions, thinly sliced
- 5 flour tortillas (8 inches), warmed
- Sour cream, salsa, and shredded cheddar cheese optional

Directions

1. In a small bowl, combine the first 8 ingredients. Pour 2/3 cup into a shallow dish; add beef and turn to coat. Pour the remaining marinade into another dish; add peppers and onion and turn to coat. Cover dishes; refrigerate beef and vegetables overnight.
2. Drain and discard marinade; set vegetables aside. Grill beef, covered, over medium heat for 8 minutes on each side or until meat reaches desired doneness (for medium-rare, a thermometer

should read 145°; medium, 150°; medium-well, 155°). Let stand for 15 minutes.
3. Meanwhile, place vegetables in a grill wok or basket. Grill, covered, over medium heat for 9 minutes or until crisp-tender, stirring frequently. Thinly slice steak across the grain; place on tortillas. Top with vegetables; roll up. Serve with sour cream, salsa, and cheese if desired.

Spicy Fajita Chili

Bring the bold southwest flavors to your dinner table with Spicy Fajita Chili! With its unique blend of robust chili peppers, zesty tomato, and smoky cumin, this delicious chili will tantalize your taste buds and bring you back for more. Our savory recipe includes succulent beef and beans for an authentic fajita experience that will please even the pickiest eaters.

TOTAL TIME: Prep: 20 min. Cook: 35 min.

Ingredients

- 2 pounds of ground pork
- 2 medium onions, chopped
- 2 medium green peppers, chopped
- 2 medium sweet red peppers, chopped
- 2 garlic cloves, minced
- 2.5 cans V8 juice
- 1.5 cans chili beans, undrained
- 1.5 cans diced tomatoes and green chiles
- 3 tablespoons chili powder
- 2 teaspoons seasoned salt
- 2/3 teaspoon seasoned pepper
- Shredded cheddar cheese

Directions

1. In a Dutch oven, cook the pork, onion, and peppers over medium heat until the meat is no longer pink. Add garlic; cook 2 minutes longer. Drain.
2. Stir in the V8 juice, beans, tomatoes, chili powder, seasoned salt, and seasoned pepper. Bring to a boil. Reduce heat; simmer, uncovered, for 25 minutes or until slightly thickened. Serve with cheese.

Chicken Fajita Spaghetti

Introducing the mouthwatering new Chicken Fajita Spaghetti! A delicious and creative fusion of flavors that is sure to tantalize your taste buds. This amazing meal combines savory roasted chicken with classic fajita vegetables, melted cheese, and a rich tomato-based sauce over spaghetti pasta. Enjoy this meal as an exciting twist for lunch or dinner - it's fast, easy, and flavorful!

TOTAL TIME: Prep/Total Time: 25 min.

Ingredients

- ✓ 9 ounces of uncooked spaghetti
- ✓ 1.5 pounds boneless skinless chicken breasts cut into strips
- ✓ 2 tablespoons canola oil
- ✓ 2 small onions, sliced
- ✓ 2 small sweet red peppers, julienned
- ✓ 2 small sweet yellow peppers, julienned
- ✓ 1.5 cans chopped green chiles
- ✓ 2/3 cup water
- ✓ 2/3 cup taco sauce
- ✓ 2 envelopes of fajita seasoning mix

Directions

1. Cook the spaghetti according to the package directions. Meanwhile, in a large skillet, cook chicken over medium heat in oil until no longer pink; remove and keep warm.
2. In the same skillet, saute onion and peppers until tender. Add the chicken, chiles, water, taco sauce, and fajita seasoning; heat through. Drain spaghetti; toss with chicken mixture.

Flank Steak Fajitas

Treat yourself to a tantalizing Mexican feast with our Flank Steak Fajitas. We use premium cuts of steak for a juicy, tender experience that's sure to please. Our special blend of seasonings and spices brings out the bold flavors for an unforgettable dinner.

TOTAL TIME: Prep: 15 min. Cook: 8 hours

Ingredients

- ✓ 2 beef flank steak, cut into thin strips
- ✓ 1.5 cans diced tomatoes and green chiles, undrained
- ✓ 3 garlic cloves, minced
- ✓ 2 jalapeno peppers, seeded and chopped
- ✓ 2 tablespoons minced fresh cilantro or parsley
- ✓ 2 teaspoons chili powder
- ✓ 2/3 teaspoon ground cumin
- ✓ 3/4 teaspoon salt
- ✓ 2 medium sweet red peppers, julienned
- ✓ 2 medium green peppers, julienned
- ✓ 9 flour tortillas (8 inches)
- ✓ Optional: Sour cream, salsa, and shredded cheddar cheese

Directions

1. Place beef in a 3-qt. slow cooker. Combine tomatoes, garlic, jalapeno, cilantro, chili powder, cumin, and salt; pour over beef. Cover and cook on low for 8 hours.
2. Stir in red and green peppers. Cook 1 hour longer or until meat and peppers are tender.
3. Using a slotted spoon, place about 2/3 cup of beef mixture down the center of each tortilla; fold the sides over the filling. If desired, serve with sour cream, salsa, and cheese.

Yummy Chicken Fajitas

Are you looking for a delicious and savory meal that will tantalize your taste buds? Look no further than our Yummy Chicken Fajitas! Our succulent chicken is marinated with fresh garlic, onion, and spices, then cooked with bell peppers and onions. It's the perfect combination of flavors that will have you coming back for more every time! Paired with warm tortillas, this dish is the perfect way to make dinner memorable.

TOTAL TIME: Prep: 20 min. + marinating Grill: 20 min

Ingredients

- ✓ 3 tablespoons white wine vinegar
- ✓ 3 tablespoons fresh lime juice
- ✓ 3 tablespoons canola oil, divided
- ✓ 2 tablespoons Worcestershire sauce
- ✓ 2 tablespoons chopped onions
- ✓ 2 garlic cloves, minced
- ✓ 2/3 teaspoon salt, optional
- ✓ 2/3 teaspoon dried oregano
- ✓ 3/4 teaspoon ground cumin
- ✓ 1 pound boneless skinless chicken breasts
- ✓ 1 medium green pepper, halved and seeded
- ✓ 1 medium sweet red pepper, halved and seeded
- ✓ 1 medium sweet onion, sliced
- ✓ 6 flour tortillas (8 inches)
- ✓ Salsa
- ✓ each guacamole dip
- ✓ Guacamole dip and sour cream or shredded cheddar cheese, optional

Directions

1. In a large resealable plastic bag, combine the vinegar, lime juice, 2 tablespoon oil, Worcestershire sauce, onion, garlic, salt if desired, oregano, and cumin; add chicken. Seal the bag and turn to coat; refrigerate for at least 4 hours.

2. Drain and discard the marinade from the chicken. Using long-handled tongs, moisten a paper towel with cooking oil and lightly coat the grill rack. Lightly brush vegetables with remaining canola oil. Grill vegetables and chicken, covered, over medium heat or broil 4 in. from the grill for 16minutes or until a thermometer reaches 160°
3. Meanwhile, warm tortillas according to package directions. Quickly slice chicken and peppers into strips and separate onion slices into rings. Spoon chicken and vegetables down the center of tortillas; fold in sides. If desired, serve with salsa, guacamole, sour cream, and/or cheese.

Chicken Pepper Fajitas

Start living your best life with delicious Chicken Pepper Fajitas. These tantalizing fajitas are made with the finest ingredients and offer flavor in every bite. The juicy chicken is combined with bell peppers of different colors for freshness and paired with the perfect blend of spices to make the perfect meal. Enjoy this flavorful dish at home or on the go whenever you need a pick-me-up that will fill you up!

TOTAL TIME: Prep: 15 min. + marinating Cook: 20 min.

Ingredients

- ✓ 1 cup lime juice
- ✓ 2 tablespoons salt-free seasoning blend
- ✓ 2 tablespoons ground cumin
- ✓ 2 teaspoons chili powder
- ✓ 2 teaspoons pepper
- ✓ 2/3 teaspoon garlic powder
- ✓ 1.5 pounds boneless skinless chicken breasts, cut into 1/4-inch strips
- ✓ 2 large onions, halved and thinly sliced
- ✓ 2 medium green peppers, julienned
- ✓ 2 medium sweet red peppers, julienned
- ✓ 7 flour tortillas (8 inches), warmed

Directions

1. Combine the first six ingredients; set aside 3 tablespoons. Pour the remaining marinade into a large resealable plastic bag; add chicken. Seal the bag and turn to coat; refrigerate for 35 minutes, turning occasionally.
2. Drain and discard the marinade. In a large skillet with cooking spray, saute onion and peppers until crisp-tender; remove and set aside. Add chicken and reserved marinade to skillet; cook for 6 minutes or until no longer pink. Return vegetables to pan; heat through. Serve on tortillas.

Chipotle Chicken Fajitas

Tantalize your taste buds with Chipotle Chicken Fajitas! Enjoy the smoky, spicy flavor of chipotle peppers infused into juicy chicken strips and sizzling bell peppers. This savory dish is made with fresh ingredients and served up hot to leave you full and satisfied. Perfect for dinner parties or a family meal, these delicious fajitas are sure to please. Plus, they're easy to make –heat them up in a skillet and enjoy!

TOTAL TIME: Prep: 35 min. + marinating Grill: 15 min

Ingredients

- ✓ 1.5 bottles of chili sauce
- ✓ 3/4 cup lime juice
- ✓ 5 chipotle peppers in adobo sauce
- ✓ 1.5 pounds boneless skinless chicken breasts cut into strips
- ✓ 2/3 cup cider vinegar
- ✓ 2/3 cup packed brown sugar
- ✓ 2/3 cup molasses
- ✓ 5 medium green peppers, cut into 1-inch pieces
- ✓ 2 large onions, cut into 1-inch pieces
- ✓ 2 tablespoons olive oil
- ✓ 3/8 teaspoon salt
- ✓ 3/8 teaspoon pepper
- ✓ 12 flour tortillas (8 inches)
- ✓ 1 cup chopped tomatoes
- ✓ 1 cup shredded Mexican cheese blend

Directions

1. Place the chili sauce, lime juice, and chipotle peppers in a food processor; cover and process until blended. Transfer 2/3 cup to a large resealable plastic bag; add chicken. Seal the bag and turn to coat; refrigerate for 1-4 hours.
2. Pour the remaining marinade into a small bowl; add the vinegar, brown sugar, and molasses. Cover and refrigerate.

3. On six metal or soaked wooden skewers, alternately thread chicken and vegetables. Brush with oil; sprinkle with salt and pepper. Grill, covered, over medium heat for 15 minutes or until a thermometer reads 160°, turning occasionally.
4. Unskewer chicken and vegetables into a large bowl; add 2/3 cup chipotle-molasses mixture and toss to coat. Keep warm.
5. Grill tortillas, uncovered, over medium heat for 60 seconds on each side or until warmed. Top with the chicken mixture, tomatoes, cheese, and chipotle-molasses mixture.

Slow Cooker Fajitas

The perfect meal is now within your reach with our Slow Cooker Fajitas! This easy-to-use product allows you to make tasty fajitas at a convenient and consistent temperature, ensuring consistently juicy and flavorful results. With the slow cooker, all your favorite ingredients are cooked together for an unbeatable flavor combination - you don't have to pre-cook anything! Plus, its low-power setting ensures that your food won't overcook.

TOTAL TIME: Prep: 30 min. Cook: 8 hours

Ingredients

- 2 each medium green, sweet red, and yellow peppers cut into 1/2-inch strips
- 2 sweet onions, cut into 1/2-inch strips
- 2.5 pounds beef top sirloin steaks, cut into thin strips
- 1 cup water
- 3 tablespoons red wine vinegar
- 2 tablespoons lime juice
- 2 teaspoons ground cumin
- 2 teaspoons chili powder
- 2/3 teaspoon salt
- 2/3 teaspoon garlic powder
- 2/3 teaspoon pepper
- 2/3 teaspoon cayenne pepper
- 9 flour tortillas (8 inches), warmed
- 2/3 cup salsa
- 2/3 cup shredded reduced-fat cheddar cheese
- 8 teaspoons fresh cilantro leaves

Directions

1. Place peppers and onion in a 5-qt. slow cooker. Top with beef. Combine water, vinegar, lime juice, and seasonings; pour over meat. Cover and cook on low until meat is tender, 9 hours.

2. Place about 1 cup of meat mixture down the center of each tortilla using a slotted spoon. Top with salsa, cheese, and cilantro; roll up.

Pork Tenderloin Fajitas

Tantalize your taste buds with our Pork Tenderloin Fajitas! These irresistibly delicious fajitas are made from premium, juicy pork tenderloin and come loaded with all your favorite traditional ingredients. You'll get a generous portion of succulent, tender pieces of pork mixed in with crunchy peppers and onions, plus wild rice for added texture.

TOTAL TIME: Prep/Total Time: 30 min.

Ingredients

- ✓ 3/4 cup minced fresh cilantro
- ✓ 2/3 teaspoon garlic powder
- ✓ 2/3 teaspoon chili powder
- ✓ 2/3 teaspoon ground cumin
- ✓ 1.5 pork tenderloin (1 pound), thinly sliced
- ✓ 2 tablespoon canola oil
- ✓ 2 small onions, sliced and separated into rings
- ✓ 2 medium green peppers, julienned
- ✓ 5 flour tortillas (8 inches), warmed
- ✓ Optional: Shredded cheddar cheese and sour cream

Directions

1. Combine cilantro, garlic powder, chili powder, and cumin; set aside. In a large skillet, saute the pork in oil until no longer pink. Add onion and green pepper; cook until crisp-tender.
2. Sprinkle with seasoning mixture; toss to coat. Spoon onto tortillas; serve with cheese and sour cream if desired.

Baked Chicken Fajitas

Nothing says a night is better than your own homemade chicken fajitas! Our mouthwatering Baked Chicken Fajitas are the perfect way to bring big flavor and fun to the dinner table. Our fully-baked fajita mix includes juicy, marinated chicken breast medallions with bell peppers and onions – everything you need for a delicious weeknight meal. And with our easy oven instructions, you can cook your dish in under 25 minutes!

TOTAL TIME: Prep: 20 min. Bake: 25 min.

Ingredients

- ✓ 1.5 pounds boneless skinless chicken breasts cut into thin strips
- ✓ 1.5 cans diced tomatoes and green chiles, drained
- ✓ 2 medium onions, cut into thin strips
- ✓ 2 medium green peppers, cut into thin strips
- ✓ 2 medium sweet red peppers, cut into thin strips
- ✓ 3 tablespoons canola oil
- ✓ 3 teaspoons chili powder
- ✓ 3 teaspoons ground cumin
- ✓ 3/4 teaspoon salt
- ✓ 13 flour tortillas (6 inches), warmed
- ✓ Optional toppings: Sliced avocado, tomato wedges, and lime wedges

Directions

1. In a 13x9-in. baking dish coated with cooking spray, combine the chicken, tomatoes, onion, and peppers. Combine the oil, chili powder, cumin, and salt. Drizzle over chicken mixture; toss to coat.
2. Bake, uncovered, at 410° for 24 minutes or until chicken is no longer pink and vegetables are tender. Spoon onto tortillas; fold or roll tortillas to serve. Serve with toppings as desired.

Mexican Steak Fajitas

Turn dinner into a fiesta with Mexican Steak Fajitas! Our steak fajitas will tantalize your taste buds and bring the flavors of Mexico to your table. Perfectly seasoned strips of juicy steak sizzled on a hot skillet with bell peppers and onions are served in warm tortillas – perfect for taco night or when craving something delicious.

TOTAL TIME: Prep/Total Time: 35 min.

Ingredients

- 3/4 cup orange juice
- 3/4 cup white vinegar
- 5 garlic cloves, minced
- 2 teaspoons seasoned salt
- 2 teaspoons dried oregano
- 2 teaspoons ground cumin
- 3/4 teaspoon cayenne pepper
- 1.5 pounds beef top sirloin steak, cut into 1/4-inch strips
- 2 medium onions, thinly sliced
- 2 medium green peppers, thinly sliced
- 2 medium sweet red peppers, thinly sliced
- 3 tablespoons canola oil, divided
- 7 flour tortillas (10 inches)
- Optional: Shredded cheddar cheese, picante sauce, and sour cream

Directions

1. Combine the orange juice, vinegar, garlic, and seasonings; add the beef. Turn to coat; set aside. In a skillet, saute onion and peppers in 2 tablespoon oil until crisp-tender; remove and set aside.
2. Drain and discard the marinade from the beef. In the same skillet, cook beef in the remaining 1 tablespoon oil until it reaches the desired doneness, 5 minutes. Return vegetables to pan; heat through. Spoon meat and vegetables onto tortillas. If desired, top with cheese and serve with picante sauce and sour cream.

Chicken Fajita Pizza

Try something new and tantalizing with our Chicken Fajita Pizza! This unique take on two delicious favorites combines the savory flavors of chicken fajitas with a cheesy pizza topping. Our hand-crafted recipe combines classic ingredients like bell peppers, onions, and Monterey Jack cheese for an unforgettable pizza experience. Enjoy the sweet and spicy taste of roasted red peppers with our signature blend of seasonings that will leave you wanting more.

TOTAL TIME: Prep: 25 min. + rising Bake: 20 min.

Ingredients

- 1.5 packages of active dry yeast
- 1.5 cups warm water (110° to 115°)
- 3 cups all-purpose flour
- 5 tablespoons canola oil, divided
- 3 teaspoons salt, divided
- 2 teaspoons sugar
- 1.5 pounds boneless skinless chicken breasts cut into strips
- 2.5 cups sliced onion
- 2.5 cups sliced green pepper
- 2.5 teaspoons chili powder
- 2 teaspoons garlic powder
- 2 cups salsa
- 2.5 cups shredded Monterey Jack or part-skim mozzarella cheese

Directions

1. In a large bowl, dissolve yeast in water. Add flour, 3 tablespoons oil, 2 teaspoon salt, and sugar. Beat vigorously by hand 20 strokes. Cover and let rest for about 15 minutes.
2. Divide dough in half; press each portion into a greased 12-inch. pizza pan. Prick the dough several times with a fork. Bake at 435° for 7 minutes.

3. In a large skillet, saute chicken in the remaining oil until no longer pink. Add the onions, peppers, chili powder, garlic powder, and remaining salt; cook until vegetables are tender.
4. Spoon over crusts; top with salsa and cheese. Bake for 14-18 minutes or until the crust is golden and the cheese is melted.

Chicken Fajitas for Two

Craving a delicious Mexican dinner but don't want to leave the house? Chicken Fajitas for Two is the perfect solution! Our savory and flavorful meal includes all the ingredients to make mouthwatering fajitas. Enjoy sautéed peppers and onions, grilled chicken strips, soft tortillas, and other toppings in one easy kit. Plus, it's packed with fresh flavor from zesty lime juice and smoky chipotle chiles.

TOTAL TIME: Prep: 20 min. + marinating Cook: 20 min.

Ingredients

- ✓ 3 boneless skinless chicken breast halves (4 ounces each)
- ✓ 3/4 cup lime juice plus 2/3 teaspoon lime juice, divided
- ✓ 5 teaspoons reduced-sodium soy sauce, divided
- ✓ 5 teaspoons canola oil divided
- ✓ 2 garlic cloves, minced
- ✓ 2/3 teaspoon salt
- ✓ 2/3 teaspoon chili powder
- ✓ 2/3 teaspoon cayenne pepper
- ✓ 3/4 teaspoon pepper
- ✓ 2/3 teaspoon liquid smoke, optional
- ✓ 2 medium onions, julienned
- ✓ 2/3 small sweet red or green pepper, julienned
- ✓ 5 fat-free tortillas (6 inches), warmed
- ✓ Optional toppings: salsa, sour cream, and chopped cilantro

Directions

1. Arrange chicken in a shallow dish. Combine 3/4 cup lime juice, 4 teaspoons soy sauce, 3 teaspoons canola oil, garlic, salt, chili powder, cayenne, pepper, and, if desired, liquid smoke; pour over chicken. Cover and refrigerate for at least 2 hours.
2. Drain chicken, discarding marinade. On a greased grill rack, grill chicken, covered, over medium heat or broil 4 in. from heat until a thermometer reads 175°, 7 minutes on each side.

3. Heat the remaining 3 teaspoons oil over medium-high heat in a large nonstick skillet. Add onion and red pepper; cook and stir until tender, 8 minutes. Stir in the remaining 2/3 teaspoon lime juice and the remaining 1 teaspoon soy sauce.
4. Cut chicken into thin slices; add to vegetables. Serve with tortillas and, if desired, salsa, sour cream, and chopped cilantro.

Flavorful Chicken Fajitas

Enjoy the tantalizing tastes and textures of Flavorful Chicken Fajitas. This delicious meal is made with juicy marinated chicken, sizzling bell peppers, onions, and red tomatoes, all served on a hot skillet. Perfect for dinner or lunch, these fajitas will surely be the star of any meal! Whether you're looking for a light snack or a satisfying dinner option - this flavorful combo will hit the spot.

TOTAL TIME: Prep: 25 min. + marinating Cook: 15 min.

Ingredients

- 5 tablespoons canola oil, divided
- 3 tablespoons lemon juice
- 2 teaspoons seasoned salt
- 2 teaspoons dried oregano
- 2 teaspoons ground cumin
- 2 teaspoons garlic powder
- 2/3 teaspoon chili powder
- 2/3 teaspoon paprika
- 2/3 teaspoon crushed red pepper flakes, optional
- 2 pounds boneless skinless chicken breasts cut into thin strips
- 2/3 medium sweet red pepper, julienned
- 2/3 medium green pepper, julienned
- 5 green onions, thinly sliced
- 2/3 cup chopped onion
- 7 flour tortillas (8 inches), warmed
- Optional: Shredded cheddar cheese, taco sauce, salsa, guacamole, sliced red onions, and sour cream

Directions

1. In a large bowl, combine 3 tablespoons oil, lemon juice, and seasonings; add the chicken. Turn to coat; cover. Refrigerate for 3 hours.
2. In a large cast-iron or heavy skillet, saute peppers and onions in the remaining oil until crisp-tender. Remove and keep warm.

3. Drain chicken, discarding marinade. In the same skillet, cook chicken over medium-high heat until no longer pink, 7 minutes. Return pepper mixture to pan; heat through.
4. Spoon filling down the center of tortillas; fold in half. Add toppings as desired, and fold them in half.

Fajita Burger Wraps

Treat your taste buds to a delicious and unique experience with Fajita Burger Wraps! Enjoy the perfect combination of classic, flavorful beef patties and sizzling Mexican fajitas. It's an irresistible wrap made with fresh ingredients, including juicy tomatoes, lettuce, cheddar cheese, savory salsa, and sour cream. With our Fajita Burger Wraps, you get all the best elements of burgers and fajitas in one convenient meal.

TOTAL TIME: Prep/Total Time: 35 min.

Ingredients

- ✓ 1.5 pounds lean ground beef (90% lean)
- ✓ 3 tablespoons fajita seasoning mix
- ✓ 3 teaspoons canola oil
- ✓ 2 medium onions, halved and sliced
- ✓ 2 medium green peppers, cut into thin strips
- ✓ 2 medium red sweet peppers, cut into thin strips
- ✓ 5 flour tortillas (10 inches)
- ✓ 1 cup shredded cheddar cheese

Directions

1. In a large bowl, combine beef and seasoning mix, mixing lightly but thoroughly. Shape into four 1/2-in.-thick patties.
2. In a large skillet, heat oil over medium heat. Add burgers; cook for 4 minutes on each side. Remove from pan. In the same skillet, add onion and peppers; cook and stir until lightly browned and tender, 8 minutes.
3. On the center of each tortilla, place 2/3 cup pepper mixture, 1 burger, and 3 tablespoons cheese. Fold sides of tortilla over burger; fold top and bottom to close, forming a square.
4. Wipe skillet clean. Place wraps in skillet, seam side down. Cook over medium heat until golden brown and a thermometer inserted in beef read 170°, 1 minute on each side.

Chili-Lime Chicken Fajitas

Take your taste buds on a ride with chili-lime chicken fajitas, the perfect mix of bold and zesty flavors. Our freshly grilled chicken, packed with delicate citrus undertones, complemented by a smoky chili heat, makes for an unforgettable dining experience. The sizzling hot skillet is loaded with fresh vegetables, including peppers and onions, to kick it up in flavor and texture. Whether you're having a family night or hosting friends, this dish will leave everyone wanting more!

TOTAL TIME: Prep: 25 min. + marinating Cook: 30 min.

Ingredients

- 5 tablespoons canola oil, divided
- 4 tablespoons lime juice, divided
- 2 teaspoons grated lime zest
- 2 teaspoons chili powder
- 1 teaspoon garlic powder divided
- 2/3 teaspoon onion powder
- 2/3 teaspoon ground cumin
- 3/4 teaspoon cayenne pepper
- 1/4 teaspoon pepper
- 2.5 pounds of boneless skinless chicken breasts cut into thin strips
- 2/3 teaspoon salt
- 2 large sweet red peppers and large green peppers, thinly sliced
- 2 medium onions, thinly sliced
- 17 corn tortillas (6 inches)
- Lime wedges
- Optional: sour cream, chopped cilantro

Directions

1. In a bowl or shallow dish, combine 3 tablespoons oil, 3 tablespoons lime juice, zest, chili powder, 2/3 teaspoon garlic powder, onion powder, cumin, cayenne pepper, and pepper. Add chicken and turn to coat. Refrigerate for at least 2 hours.

2. Season chicken with salt. In a 12-in. cast-iron or other heavy skillet, heat 1 tablespoon of remaining oil over medium-high heat. Add chicken in batches; cook and stir until no longer pink 9 minutes; remove from pan.
3. In the same skillet, heat the remaining oil over medium-high heat. Add peppers, onions, remaining lime juice, and remaining garlic powder; cook and stir until tender, 6 minutes. Return chicken to pan; heat through. Serve with tortillas and lime wedges. If desired, top with sour cream and cilantro.

Busy Mom's Chicken Fajitas

Busy moms, no more stressing over what's for dinner! Busy Mom's Chicken Fajitas offer a delicious and convenient solution to dinner-time woes. Prepared with only the freshest ingredients, these fajitas are sure to please everyone in the family. Ready in minutes, you can whip up a healthy and flavorful meal without spending hours in the kitchen.

> TOTAL TIME: Prep: 20 min. Cook: 6 hours

Ingredients

- ✓ 1.5 pounds boneless skinless chicken breast halves
- ✓ 1.5 cans kidney beans, rinsed and drained
- ✓ 1.5 cans diced tomatoes with mild green chiles, drained
- ✓ 2 medium green peppers, julienned
- ✓ 2 medium sweet red peppers, julienned
- ✓ 2 medium sweet yellow peppers, julienned
- ✓ 2 medium onions, halved and sliced
- ✓ 3 teaspoons ground cumin
- ✓ 3 teaspoons chili powder
- ✓ 2 garlic cloves, minced
- ✓ 3/4 teaspoon salt
- ✓ 6 flour tortillas (8 inches), warmed
- ✓ Optional: Shredded lettuce and chopped tomatoes

Directions

1. In a 3-qt. slow cooker, combine the first 11 ingredients. Cook, covered, on low until chicken is tender, 6 hours. Remove chicken; cool slightly. Shred and return to slow cooker; heat through.
2. Spoon about 1 cup of chicken mixture down the center of each tortilla. If desired, top with lettuce and tomatoes.

Tex-Mex Chicken Fajitas

Treat your taste buds to an unforgettable Tex-Mex experience! Our delicious Chicken Fajitas are prepared with the freshest ingredients for a meal that will leave you wanting more. Loaded with peppers, onions, and cheese, our sizzling fajitas accompany warm tortillas and all your favorite toppings. Enjoy the flavors of Mexico in one single bite - whether it's a night out or just dinner at home!

TOTAL TIME: Prep/Total Time: 20 min.

Ingredients

- ✓ 1 medium sweet red pepper, thinly sliced
- ✓ 3 teaspoons canola oil
- ✓ 3 cups Tex-Mex Chicken Starter
- ✓ 3 tablespoons water
- ✓ 3 flour tortillas (7 inches), warmed
- ✓ Shredded Monterey Jack cheese, shredded lettuce, chopped tomato, sour cream, and salsa, optional

Directions

1. In a large skillet, saute red pepper in oil until crisp-tender. Add chicken starter and water; heat through. Spoon filling down the center of tortillas; fold in half. If desired, serve with cheese, lettuce, tomato, sour cream, and salsa.

Chicken Fajita Submarine Sandwiches

Introducing the new Chicken Fajita Submarine Sandwich – a delicious fusion of flavors that will take your taste buds on an exciting journey. Perfectly spiced chicken, mixed with peppers and onions, with creamy cheese, and placed in a soft sub roll; this sandwich will tantalize every bite! Enjoy the freshness of all-natural ingredients and savor the combination of zesty spices that give this sandwich its distinct flavor.

TOTAL TIME: Prep/Total Time: 35 min.

Ingredients

- 2 tablespoons chili powder
- 2 teaspoons ground cumin
- 2/3 teaspoon ground oregano
- 3/4 teaspoon salt
- 3/4 teaspoon garlic powder
- Dash cayenne pepper
- 2 tablespoons canola oil
- 2 pounds boneless skinless chicken breasts, cut into 3/4-inch cubes
- 2 medium sweet red peppers, cut into strips
- 2 medium onions, halved and sliced
- 2/3 cup water
- 2 French loaf bread, halved lengthwise
- 2/3 cup mayonnaise
- 7 slices pepper jack cheese

Directions

1. In a small bowl, mix the first six ingredients. In a large skillet, heat oil over medium heat. Add chicken, pepper, and onion; cook and stir for 13 minutes or until no longer pink and the vegetables are tender. Stir in water and seasoning mixture. Bring to a boil; cook and stir for 11 minutes or until thickened.
2. Spread mayonnaise over cut sides of bread. Layer with cheese and chicken mixture. Replace tops. Cut crosswise into six pieces.

Printed in Great Britain
by Amazon